The Greater Call

MY ENCOUNTER

Denelse Fearon

Published by:

DAYELight
PUBLISHERS

ISBN: 978-1-949343-85-4 (paperback)

Unless otherwise stated, Scripture quotations marked KJV are from the Holy Bible, King James Version (Authorized Version). First published in 1611. Quoted from the KJV Classic Reference Bible, Copyright 1983, by The Zondervan Corporation.

Table of Contents

Acknowledgement

I must give honour and thanks to my Abba Father in Heaven; thank You for entrusting me with the privilege, gift and desire to write this devotional book. I am humbled that You have chosen me as one of Your vessels to bless Your people.

To my husband, daughter and siblings, thank you for believing in me; and motivating me through the journey of life and as I wrote this book. I love you and I am grateful to God for you.

To all my friends, supporters, well-wishers, and prayer warriors, thank you.

To my editor, proof-readers, graphic designers and all those who helped in making this devotional book a reality; I am grateful for you all.

God bless you!

Introduction

I have written the Greater Call to propel you into pursuing the call of God upon your life.

The content of this book gives an account of my personal experience with the Lord. It is also scripture-based encouragement, which will boost your momentum during the different seasons on this journey of fulfilling the call of God upon your life.

I was inspired to write this book out of great concern that people are so busy fulfilling their desired goals, to pay attention to God's greater call for their lives. The fact is, many people believe their accomplishment in life settles it for them. However, in reality, God has an intended purpose for us all. With that being said, I want to highlight that your personal accomplishment/job is not necessarily your divine purpose on earth.

On a spiritual level, there are people who are spectators in church; people who have not made themselves useful in enhancing the kingdom of God, because they are ignorant of their giftings. God's will for us is to use the gift He has placed within us to enhance His Kingdom, for His glory.

Jesus Christ taught us this fact through the parable of the talents (See Matthew 25:14-30).

It is my prayer that as you read this book, you will be convicted by the Holy Spirit to step out boldly and deliberately to your greater call.

The Encounter

We are all created in the likeness and image of God. We are all unique and were created for different purposes.

So God created man in his own image, in the image of God created he him; male and female created he them. (Genesis 1:27).

From a very tender age, I knew there was something different and unique about me. There were certain things I could not do; even if I gave it my best try, it would feel off and odd. I was an obedient child, in most instances; I would try my best to do the things that seemed good. I loved going to church and, to make it better, I was living right next door to the church I grew up in.

It was also a pleasure to go by the church building on Saturday evenings, after a long day of doing chores. I would help with the cleaning for Sunday morning worship services. Those days were exciting and full of fun.

Having grown up in the church environment, I soon gave my life to the Lord and was baptised at the age of seventeen (17) years old. Church life, for me then, was much fun. I enjoyed every moment of it. Soon after, I became very active in the church; I worked in different departments.

Naturally, as a teenager transitioning into adulthood, I was faced with many struggles. I have to admit that I wasn't perfect, but I tried my best.

And he said unto me, My grace is sufficient for thee: for my strength is made perfect in weakness. Most gladly therefore will I rather glory in my infirmities, that the power of Christ may rest upon me. (2 Corinthians 12:9).

Later on, in my Christian journey, I began to experience God in a different way. I loved to pray, and I still believe that prayer could be the reason for this new experience with God. I developed a great passion to do the work of the Lord; I really wanted to make myself available and obedient. I am an introvert; and therefore, though the desire to serve in God's kingdom was there, I held back myself for many years. I thought I was too quiet to really step out into what God had called me to do. Many years passed by, but my new experiences with God and my desire to serve Him did not change.

However, I convinced myself that this could not be the journey for me. Besides, there were so many other things that I saw myself doing. I simply wanted to be saved, go to church and live an exemplary Christian life, all in an effort to avoid going to hell, but that was just about it.

I was busy doing my own thing and I thought everything was fine. I became comfortable pursuing myself and my goals. In the midst of all this comfort, the Lord began to minister to me in various ways. I could not resist the call anymore; I found myself in a position where I had to choose to do what God had called me to do.

The year 2011 was a very interesting year for me; it was the year I thought I would begin to fulfil my call. I answered yes to the Lord, "Yes Lord, I will do anything that you require of me." However, deep down, I only meant it to an extent. The Lord must have been laughing at me because He knows the intent and desires of our hearts, even when we attempt to conceal them in counterfeit utterances.

The Audible Voice of God

From 2011- 2015 I did little things for God. I was bent on not doing anything too major; I really did not want to put myself out there. All I wanted was to stay in my small corner and only impact whomever 'set foot' in it.

If you read my first book titled "Faith in the Midst of Adversity", you will remember that 2015 was a particularly challenging year for me. It was in that year I began to seek God in a different way. As I began to know Him better, I started to hear Him speak profoundly to me. It was always an awesome experience. In the awesomeness of this experience, I felt this awareness that I may not quite hit the mark in my limited human ability. I was therefore aware that I had to submit totally to Him. I surrendered everything: my own will and desires.

One morning, in the year 2016, the month of July, my daughter was being taken to summer school by her dad to prepare for her G-SAT examination the following year. When they left and I was left alone at home, I lay on my back in bed as I prepared to take a nap. As I lay there and stared into the ceiling, waiting to fall asleep, something unusual began to happen; allow me to describe it as best as possible:

I felt as though I was in a strange place; I could not hear anything or see anything around me. The ceiling then seemed to turn into a big screen, and I began to watch a movie; it continued for about 45 minutes. As soon as I finished and was about to get back to myself, I heard a voice saying, "Acts Chapter 2." I quickly realised that it was the voice of the Lord. I began to cry out to Him asking, "What are you saying Lord? I really don't understand." At that moment, my husband opened the door and walked into the house. I was stunned and excited. I couldn't wait to tell him what had just happened, so I called out to him to come to the bedroom and I began to share my experience. Afterwards, I asked him to read Acts Chapter 2 for me. As I listened, I noticed that it was very similar to the vision I had seen earlier. I broke down in tears and began to pray as I asked the Lord for a revelation of what He was doing. That very night, I was in prayer. It was after this prayer session that the Lord began to speak to me. He said, "Prophesy to your husband." There wasn't enough time to think about what I heard; God began to speak to my husband through me. I then went straight to bed after that, with a feeling of contentment that my task for the day was accomplished. The word which the Lord had spoken to my husband through me, was confirmed with a phone call we received the following morning.

The Prophetic Call

The prophetic call on my life was manifested when the Lord spoke to me and said He would release the prophetic fire upon my life (See Jeremiah 20:9).

I had rejected and doubted this call on many occasions, but the Lord firmly but gracefully reminded me of His call every time I sought after Him.

I couldn't help myself: as I prayed and ministered to people, I would begin to prophesy over their lives. God began to reveal things to me, and I would speak to them as He gave me the utterance to do so.

I remember one day I was on a call with a friend, who lived in the Cayman Island. As we spoke, she told me that she would like me to pray with her concerning a particular situation. I began to pray and, as I was praying, the Lord began to give me revelations and spoke to me concerning the situation she had. He gave me the utterance to prophesy to her. She was amazed; she began to ask how I knew this.

There was another instance when I was praying with a group of people and the Lord began to give me the utterance to prophesy to them one by one.

The Word of God declares that He is a revealer of secrets and the prophetic is one way in which He does this (See Daniel 2:28).

As I operated in the prophetic, I began to question myself and God. I was afraid and wanted to ensure that this prophetic gift wasn't born of self but of the Holy Spirit. In my heart, I felt like I would rather be an ordinary servant and make it into heaven, than to be a false prophet and not make it.

I cried many days and nights as the prophetic became very pronounced in my life. There was this particular day as I questioned God about it, I had the same experience as the day I received my calling, while I was at home laying on my back in bed. This time, I was placed in a trance and I heard the voice of the Lord speaking to me. He said, "I will take ordinary men and make them extra-ordinary." I then came back to my senses and began to worship Him.

There was a time I was invited to a prayer meeting on a Wednesday night. As I entered the room, my attention was drawn to a young lady who was also in the meeting. I kept staring at her; I couldn't help what the Holy Spirit was doing. As I stared at her, the Lord began to speak to me concerning what was happening to her. He told me that she was bound by witchcraft, and she was having issues with her stomach. As I received this revelation, I began speaking back to the Lord, "Why are you doing this, Lord? It is my first time here and I really don't want to seem too noticeable or for anyone to get the impression that I want to take over the meeting." That did not change the mind of God. In fact, He spoke even more. He told me to lay my hands on the woman's stomach and pray for her. I became uncomfortable for a while as I wrestled with the instructions I received. Soon after, the Lord provided the opportunity for me to do what He had instructed me to. I lay my hand on the woman's stomach and, as I began praying, the Spirit of the Lord took over. The woman began to cry and scream as the hand of God began to operate in her stomach. She was relieved of the terrible pain and discomfort she was suffering from. She left the prayer meeting delivered.

The following week, she returned to the meeting to share her testimony of how she was delivered. She was grateful and gave praises unto God.

As my journey into the prophetic continued, and as I operated as the Lord led, I was still concerned about my actions and so I continued to ask God some questions. I remember, on more than one occasion, I was prophesied to that the Lord has called me to be a prophet, but I didn't take it seriously. I thought it couldn't be true; I even thought about how people would ridicule me and say all manner of things against me. I could identify with the fears of Moses at the burning bush. I knew that for as long as one is called of God, especially to the office of a prophet, it attracts the harsh judgement and ridicule of many. I was very afraid of this.

I remember in 2017, I was in a foreign land, visiting with a friend. One Tuesday, I was alone at my friend's home, so I decided that it was a good time to have a talk with the Lord. As I got myself ready to engage in the conversation, I decided that I would start it off with some worship. I therefore grabbed my phone and went straight to YouTube. As I opened it, the song "Your Grace and Mercy" was at the top of the list; I tapped on it for it to play. As the song began to play, tears began to flow from my eyes uncontrollably and I started to worship God. My heart was filled with gratitude. I worshipped into prayer and, soon after, I started to ask the Lord some questions: "Are You serious about this? What is it that You will have me to do?"

I began to tell Him how afraid I was and that I needed Him to respond in that moment to reassure me of what He had already confirmed numerous times before. I listened for His response and, as I waited, I heard the voice of the Lord speaking to me. He said, "Read Jeremiah Chapter 1." I rushed for my Bible and began to read the chapter. As I read it, it resonated with my spirit. Through this word, I heard God saying, "I called you just as I called the prophet

Jeremiah." I took heed of the call once more and kept on reading this chapter for weeks. I concluded the study on the book of Jeremiah; this was very important to me.

A few months later, I was standing in my kitchen feeling perplexed again. *Is this call for real?* I pondered to myself. As soon as I was about to convince myself that it wasn't real, I heard the same voice say: "Remember, I gave you Jeremiah Chapter 1." I had to apologise to the Lord for allowing negative thoughts to consume my mind.

Get Out of the Noise and the Crowd

I was working at a particular business place and I was enjoying every moment of it. I soon became comfortable and thought I would settle there for a while. I became so dedicated and just wanted to get my job done. I was there for a time; but one day I heard God speaking in my spirit saying, "Your time is up. It's time to go." I thought about it for a moment, but then a few days later, I paid no attention to it. "Maybe that was just my mind," I tried to convince myself.

A few weeks passed and I heard nothing, so I started to make myself comfortable again. One night, not very long afterwards, I was lying in bed and was reminiscing on the day's activity. The voice of the Lord began to speak to me about what He said to me a few weeks earlier. I became so restless and uncomfortable as He spoke. It felt like a mother scolding her child: "This is not what I called you to do. That is not the place for you," He said. I began to cry and told Him to just let me finish that month and then I would go. As I shared the news that I was going to leave, I was ridiculed, looked on as stupid and the list goes on. So many people had a lot to say. I became very angry with God: "How could you tell me to do this only for me to get humiliated, belittled and bashed by people's words."

I argued in my spirit with Him. Then I heard the voice of the Lord saying: "You act as a dog returning to its vomit." As He spoke to me, the Spirit of the Lord came upon me. I began to speak in a language that I have never spoken before. It was an unusual utterance. I prayed and asked for His pardon. I decided that I would never look back, and I would be obedient to God.

Sometimes we find ourselves in a crowd, and God may be saying that this is not the place for you, and you may question this. I want you to know that when God uproots you from a place, it doesn't mean that the people surrounding you are bad, it just means that He wants to plant you where He has called you to be. The noise in the environment that you are in may be too loud for you to hear Him speak. You may become too busy to hear Him when He speaks. Sometimes the plans we have for our lives are great, but the plan that God has for us is far greater.

Purification

The process of purification is a daily thing where you ask God to cleanse your heart in order for you to please Him.

But as he which hath called you is holy, so be ye holy in all manner of conversation; because it is written, Be ye holy; for I am holy." (1 Peter 1:15-16).

As you answer the call of God upon your life, you will go through purification. The submission of your spirit to God is the most important thing during purification. In order to acquire virtue, you must be humble and careful, so that you can detect when your life is going contrary to the will of God. It is at this point that you pray to Him to help you come into alignment with His will for your life.

Christ wants us to completely submit our will to His. Purification requires the soul to be pure and clean of your own will. You will spiritually progress when you allow your will to be fully submitted to God's will. When your will is completely submitted to God's will, to identically match God's will, your soul will be cleansed and the will of God will govern your life.

The more you purify yourself, the more you allow for divine grace to function with authority in your life. When a soul is completely clean from its own will, and is totally humbled, then it can experience the grace of Christ and the fulfilment of all His promises. It is at this point that you will begin to operate in His call for you.

But in a great house there are not only vessels of gold and of silver, but also of wood and of earth; and some to honour, and some to dishonour. If a man therefore purge himself from these, he shall be a vessel unto honour, sanctified, and meet for the master's use, and prepared unto every good work." (2 Timothy 2:20-21).

We are not condemned because of our sinful nature but by our own will, which opposes God's will. When we approve the will of God for our lives, our souls are kept safe from destruction and hopelessness through the seasons of life.

Wherefore let them that suffer according to the will of God commit the keeping of their souls to him in well doing, as unto a faithful Creator. (1 Peter 4:19).

And he said to them all, If any man will come after me, let him deny himself, and take up his cross daily, and follow me. (Luke 9:23).

In my devotional titled "Faith in the Midst of Adversity," I wrote about how I was disappointed with God after losing my mom suddenly. I decided that I would not be praying for people anymore, because I felt that the time when I needed God to show up for me the most, He did not. I was later reminded that when the call of God is upon your life, and you truly desire to please Him, it is never about you, but totally denying yourself and being willing and obedient to His will. I knew that part of what God had called me to do was to intercede for His people; but because I was hurting, I thought I could spite God right back by going against His will. Listen up! You can never spite God but yourself; because when you stray from Him, your life will be damned, but He will remain God. Hurt can sometimes cause you to stray from God's will but be reminded that true peace and healing comes from surrendering all to Him and being obedient to His call.

Sanctification

For all have sinned, and come short of the glory of God. (Romans 3:23).

Sanctification is the state of proper functioning. To sanctify someone or something is to set that person apart for the use intended. You are sanctified when you live according to God's purpose. You cannot sanctify yourself, only God sanctifies. In 2 Corinthians 7:1, Paul calls for trust and obedience to be active in the life of a believer when he says, *"Having therefore these promises, dearly beloved, let us cleanse ourselves from all filthiness of the flesh and spirit, perfecting holiness in the fear of God."*

The Holy Spirit plays a key role in the process of sanctification. As we walk in the power of the Spirit, we will not gratify the desires of the flesh (See Galatians 5:16). God empowers us through His Spirit, but He also gives us some tools to help us through the process of sanctification:

- Reading and studying the Word of God, which will equip us to fully understand who God is and be better able to function in our calling.

- Fellowship with other believers.

- Praying and expressing our faith and the sovereignty of our God.

- Valuing God's work and His call on our lives more than our own fleshy desires.

- Becoming active by sharing the Word of God and use them to guide us as ministers in our capacity.

God is exceedingly interested in helping us to go forward through sanctification. Our part is to want it, to acknowledge our need for it and then launch out in obedience to God's Word and the Holy Spirit in faith.

Philippians 1:6 says, *"Being confident of this very thing, that he which hath begun a good work in you will perform it until the day of Jesus Christ."*

The Assignment

As I get out of the crowd and the noise, I was able to wait and listen. I knew God was taking me on a journey. I had many assignments that I had to complete, so I waited and made myself available for each one.

In particular seasons of my life, it was different. I was given the task of ministering and guiding young Christian women on their spiritual journey with the Lord. I paused to ask the Lord what He was doing. I always wanted to be sure that this was God's doing and nothing of myself. I often asked, "Lord, why would You do this, when I too need someone to guide me on my spiritual journey?" My relationship with the Lord was a great one and so there was not a time that I spoke to Him or asked Him questions, without His response. The Lord assured me that He had given me this assignment. I was humbled to know that for yet another time, He chose me when I knew I was unworthy. He made me worthy.

At some point in my calling, the Lord called me to minister to young ladies. He assigned me to a young lady for a season. I was tasked with praying, counselling, and sharing His Word with each one. In whatever challenge they had spiritually, I had to guide them with the help of the Holy Spirit to overcome. This was like a daily routine for me. This continued for a while, then the Lord released me to move on to other assignments.

In this chapter, I really don't want to focus on the assignments that God entrusted me with. Rather, I would like you to know that each of us are called to a specific assignment. Some assignments may be long-term, while some may be just for a season. Jeremiah was called as a prophet to the nations. Elijah was also called as a prophet and there are so many others that I could speak about.

The book of 1 Corinthians 12:12-27, speaks of one body with many members. Therefore, it means that everyone cannot serve in the same office of ministry. Some had to be called as an apostle, pastor, teacher, etc. Also, everyone is not blessed with the same gifts; some are blessed with the gifts of giving, healing, diversities of tongues, etc.

The point I am trying to make is, be appreciative of your gift or the office you have been called into in the body of Christ. Many times, we get distracted and tend to be fixated on the gifts and calling of others, rather than being focused or being intentional about the task God has given us to do. All offices and gifts are important because they work together to achieve one main goal: and that is to equip, empower, edify and save souls for the Kingdom of God.

My questions to you are:

- What are you called to do?
- What is your gift?
- Are you being intentional about doing the will of God?
- Have you lost focus?
- What are you doing about it?
- What are you doing with what God has blessed you with?

As you reflect on these questions, I want to challenge you to be focused on the call God has placed on your life, the giftings He has blessed you with and use them accordingly to His glory and the advancement of His Kingdom.

Understanding the Prophetic
Being Released into the Prophetic

I remember in April 2004, I was preparing for my wedding on the 10th. As I came home from school, tired and exhausted, I decided that I was going to take a rest. As I lay on my bed and waited to fall asleep, something unique happened. It was as though I was watching a movie; I saw my husband-to-be being shot in the arm. Soon after, I came back to my senses. I wondered for a moment what that was and if that could really be true. With little knowledge of the prophetic then, I did not understand that God was sharing this to me.

I was still going on in my walk with the Lord and did not understand many things. As a result, I did nothing about what I saw. A few days later, the vision I had come to pass. My husband called to say that he had been shot, three days before our wedding day. I was devastated; I blamed myself. I was bitter and fearful in the whole situation. I thought it was all my fault. I should have prayed and cancelled the plan of the enemy.

Understanding the prophetic is very important. When God reveals anything to you, seek His instruction, then act immediately. I was lacking in knowledge then; and as a result, the enemy gained access to our lives. The Word of God declares in Isaiah 5:13: *"Therefore my people are gone into captivity, because they have no knowledge: and their honourable men are famished, and their multitude dried up with thirst."*

Amos 3:7-8 says: *Surely the Lord God will do nothing, but he revealeth his secret unto his servants the prophets. The lion hath roared, who will not fear? the Lord God hath spoken, who can but prophesy?*

The prophetic ministry is one of the many ways by which God speaks to His people. God is sovereign and whatever He does is well done. God has chosen to use people on the earth as His mouthpiece; such are called prophets. God reveals His secret things to His servants, the prophets, and there are various ways in which this is being done. When God speaks to the prophet, he has no choice but to prophesy. As prophets, when God speaks, His prophetic words are like burning fire within us, which must be released to those it is intended for. We must act according to His divine instructions.

Some of the ways God speaks in the prophetic are through dreams, visions, His audible voice, etc. Hosea 12:10 says, *"I have also spoken by the prophets, and I have multiplied visions, and used similitudes, by the ministry of the prophets."* Visions represent something that is "seen." This could be sight into the spirit realm: seeing a picture that comes to the prophet's mind. This picture could be presented or shown to the physical eyes. This could happen while awake, in a trance; or when asleep, through a dream.

The Audible Voice of God

God spoke audibly to people and He is still speaking this way. The audible voice of God is a spiritual voice that only the people to whom God is speaking to hear it, while those who are not in His intended audience will not hear what He is saying.

The audible voice of God is real and clear. It can be as though there is another person standing right next to you and speaking to you, yet others around you may not hear. In 1 Samuel 3:2-9, Samuel heard the Lord, while Eli did not.

God's Spirit is awesome and amazing in His workings. The Holy Spirit operates in unusual and creative ways to convey the thoughts/mind of God. God conveys His messages in a combination of different ways. Consider Jeremiah at the potter's house: Jeremiah heard God's Word as God used the natural process of a potter working at his wheel to convey His plan for a nation.

On Another Level

As you grow in faith and in your spiritual walk with the Lord, there will be different stages of growth and maturity. As you grow, you will become selfless. You will develop an increased level of faith, which will be able to discern the voice of God, and you will not be afraid to boldly declare the Word or the mind of Christ.

In my early years as a Christian, I was bombarded with fear and lack of confidence. I believed that what others thought of me mattered, so I was therefore silent, opting not to declare many things that God has revealed and placed on my heart. Isaiah 43:1 says: *"But now thus saith the Lord that created thee, O Jacob, and he that formed thee, O Israel, Fear not: for I have redeemed thee, I have called thee by thy name; thou art mine."* God actually commands us not to fear.

As I grew in God and accepted the call He placed on my life, I became bold and selfless. I know now that I am not my own and I belong to Jesus. I am totally His and whatever He commands me to do is obligatory to me. As I operate in the prophetic, there are many times that I am asked to share. Without hesitation, I have become bold enough to declare the mind of Christ and to release the Word. He impressed it on my heart to minister to His people, without fear or compromise.

There are many areas in our faith walk that growth is expected, for example, prayer life, studying the Word, etc. It can be very distressful and irritating when one becomes stagnant in their spiritual growth. God wants us to grow from one level to the next, so that His glory may be manifested in and through us. 2 Peter 3:18 says, *"But grow in grace, and in the knowledge of our Lord and Saviour Jesus Christ. To him be glory both now and for ever. Amen."*

I have a few questions for you to reflect on:

- What are your struggles spiritually?
- What areas of your spiritual walk do you desire to grow in?
- Are you ready to move to another level in Him?

I challenge you today that as you meditate on these questions, you will seek to grow in faith and grace, and you will know you are called as an ambassador/servant of God. You have a purpose you are called to fulfil for such a time as this. Strive to operate in the capacity of your calling and let the kingdom of God be exalted.

The Challenges

There will be many challenges as you strive to grow in grace and in the knowledge of the Lord Jesus Christ. Jesus Himself was tempted by satan; you are certainly not an exception (See Matthew 4:1-11). Jesus used the Word to defeat satan. He studied the Word diligently from His childhood. There is therefore no excuse to not study the Word of God, for this is the weapon of mass destruction against satan and his agents.

Let me give you a personal experience where I was deeply challenged in my spiritual growth. I can remember this particular time I was bombarded with so many struggles that it seemed like there was no light at the end of the tunnel. My journey was a devastating one, and I was at the point where I felt like giving up on the divine call that was upon my life. I decided that I did not want to hear from God anymore, I was just done with this.

Sometimes I was called to minister to others in order for them to overcome and get delivered from the same challenges I was facing; it was not easy. At some point, I became adamant that I would not go any further with this call on my life. I prayed continuously for myself and my family, but I was not interested in hearing from God about anyone and their struggles. During this time, as I recall, God spoke to me concerning a young church sister and her family. He told me that I should pray for them; but I wasn't interested. A few days passed, and I was still disobedient. Still being in the mindset of not wanting to hear from God, I received a call from the same sister; she told me that her son was shot. In my stunned state, I quickly inquired if he was dead. I felt so bad and disturbed because the Lord spoke to me concerning them, but because I was rebellious, I did not intercede on their behalf. After I found out that he was still alive, I began to intercede on his behalf, asking God to spare his life. During my intercession for him, I became convicted by the Holy Spirit. I was deeply touched and vowed that I would always do what God required of me.

What are some challenges you are bombarded with as you continue on this spiritual journey? Write them down, present them to God and He will reveal to you, through His Word or His servants, how you will overcome.

Study To Show Thyself Approved

When you answer the call of God upon your life, and you strive to grow spiritually, you must study His Word in order to know Him and to be able to discern His voice. 2 Timothy 2:15 says, *"Study to shew thyself approved unto God, a workman that needeth not to be ashamed, rightly dividing the word of truth."*

As I sought the Lord continuously, the Lord instructed me to start studying His Word. I heard His voice speaking to me audibly. He asked, "How will you prophecy, how will you preach to the people, if you don't know My Word?" Without hesitation, I formed a Bible study group with some other sisters who were hungry for the Word of God as well. As I began to study His Word, it felt like food to my hungry soul. My desire for the Word of God was heightened. As I continued to study, the Lord began to reveal Himself to me through His Word. I received many revelations and my gift was activated to another level. I was now able to function more effectively and efficiently as I continued to do the work of the Lord.

Some of the benefits of studying God's Word are:

- It gives life both spiritually and physically. (See Psalm 119:25, 50).

- Helps you grow in faith and in Christlikeness. (See Romans 10:17).

- It matures you so you can lead others in truth. (See 2 Timothy 3:16-17).

- It helps you to fight spiritual battles and experience victory. (See Matthew 4:1-4).

- It gives you peace and hope. (See Philippian 4:8-9).

- It helps us to produce spiritual fruits. (See Psalm 1:2-3).

I encourage you, my friend, do not neglect the potential power of God's Word in your life and spiritual growth. It is immeasurable and indescribable.

Staying in God's Presence

My appetite for the things of God, and my desire to know Him deeper, began to grow even more. I wanted to stay in His presence. Staying in God's presence can be difficult at times. You may find yourself distracted by the cares of life and many things that the devil may bring against you. You must be aware of these factors and ask the Lord to teach/help you to remain focus and stay in His presence. I will not tell you that I got it all right in the beginning, but I was sincere in my journey and decided that whatever the challenges were, I would remain focused. I was aware of my calling and I knew that I must remain faithful. I decided to please God.

In order for you to stay in God's presence, you must renew your mind daily. Your mind is a very important part of your body. This is where you reason; this is where you make decisions and therefore it is the battlefield. In the mind is where doubt attacks. It is also where fear first comes in. It is very important to fill your mind with the Word of God. The Word of God is powerful; it will break the bondage of doubt and fear (See Romans 12:1-2).

You can get your mind renewed in these ways:

- Read the Word of God.
- Meditate on the Word of God.
- Memorize the Word of God.

The Bible tells us that the Holy Spirit is our Helper. He will constantly remind you of what you should do, similar to a computer storing the truth in your mind (See John 14:26). When you are faced with temptation, the Holy Spirit will remind you, so you will have the strength to go through/overcome. Sometimes your thoughts and feelings can be very deceitful, and that is why you need to constantly renew your mind.

Staying in God's Will

Proverbs 3:5-6 says, *"Trust in the Lord with all thine heart; and lean not unto thine own understanding. In all thy ways acknowledge him, and he shall direct thy paths."*

I can tell you that staying in God's will is not a walk in the park. It takes a daily, conscious and deliberate effort of submitting yourself to Him. You must be intentional about seeking His guidance so that His will may be done in you.

Often times, our own will and what we desire is not aligned with the will of God for our lives. However, we must recognize that God's will for our lives is perfect and it will propel us into fulfilling His call on our lives.

I can recall many times when my Christian journey, and the trials that came with it, seemed very contrary to what the Word of God declares. It would cause me to perceive giving up and discontinuing the journey of my calling as the best and most realistic option. "At least I will be relieved from the battles I am faced with," I often thought to myself. God does not desire us to give up; rather, like Jacob, He desires for us to wrestle with Him daily through prayer, until we have received what He has in store for our lives (See Genesis

32:22-31). "How do I stay in God's Word?" is a question that you may ask. Here are some key points to staying in God's will:

1. Building a relationship with Him. Once you are a believer, you must seek to build a relationship with God through prayer. God requires a relationship rather than religion. When you commune and become intimate with Him, God will begin to reveal His plan for you.

2. Presenting your body as a living sacrifice (See Romans 12). Be willing to give up activities, habits, lifestyles and friends that are not pleasing to the Lord. You must decide daily to be obedient to God's Word.

3. Be deliberate about the use of your gift for the advancement of the Kingdom of God (See Romans 12:6). Every individual is blessed with different gifts; and every gift is important to the body of Christ. Do not be jealous of another person's gift. Instead, find your place in God's service and work your gift in humility and faith.

4. Building each other up (See 1 Thessalonians 5:11). Helping others to become successful in their calling, and building others up, is one of the most fulfilling things you can do in Christendom. It serves to form

a strong support network in ministry, and it pleases God.

5. Ask God to increase your faith daily (See Hebrews 11). Without faith we cannot please God. However, if we seek Him, He will reward us. The will of God becomes obvious only by possession of faith and the application of God's Word in our daily lives. Acknowledge God in all your ways and seek Him wholeheartedly, and you will, by His grace, stay in His will.

Being Ridiculed

Once you are a believer in Jesus Christ, and you have accepted Him as your Lord and Saviour, be reminded that you will be ridiculed and talked about in the worst of ways. Paul the Apostle was a true and dedicated servant of Jesus Christ, who went about preaching and teaching about Him. He was also a persecutor of the church at one point in His life; he would ensure that Christians were killed. When Paul got converted and began doing the work of the Lord, he was talked about in the worst way because of His past life.

Many people are afraid to own and fulfil the call of God on their lives because of what people might say about them. If God has called and approved you, it doesn't matter what people will say. 2 Timothy 2:15 says, *"Study to shew thyself approved unto God, a workman that needeth not to be ashamed, rightly dividing the word of truth."* 1 Peter 4:14 also says, *"If ye be reproached for the name of Christ, happy are ye; for the spirit of glory and of God resteth upon you: on their part he is evil spoken of, but on your part he is glorified."*

I want to encourage you to be intentional about who God has called you to be. Work the gift He has blessed you with to the best of your ability.

Humility in God

1 Peter 4:10-11 says, *"As every man hath received the gift, even so minister the same one to another, as good stewards of the manifold grace of God. If any man speak, let him speak as the oracles of God; if any man minister, let him do it as of the ability which God giveth: that God in all things may be glorified through Jesus Christ, to whom be praise and dominion for ever and ever. Amen."*

God desires to be able to use us for His glory and His purpose; we must recognize this. Humility requires us to use our gifts and capabilities under God's instruction and guidance, and always giving Him the glory and honour for what is accomplished.

We must never allow ourselves to indulge in self-pride because of the manifestation of God's gift in us. Rather, we must remain humble and mindful that we are servants of Jesus Christ. Jesus Christ, though He is God, came to earth as a servant in the likeness of men (See Philippians 2:7-8). Jesus is our ultimate example: He gave up His own will so the will of His father could be done; He gave up His life to be crucified for our sins. We must adopt the humility of

Jesus Christ in order for us to serve His flock. We must forsake our own will and reputation, in order to be obedient to God's Word and will. When we humble ourselves under the mighty hand of God, we grow in grace and in our Christian walk. If you are humble, then you are ready to fulfil God's plan for your life, and God will strengthen you. God strengthens those who desire to live unto His honour and glory (See Isaiah 66:1-2).

How to Discover Your God-Given Purpose

Psalm 57:2 says, *"I will cry unto God most high; unto God that performeth all things for me."* This verse of Scripture speaks volumes. It is key in understanding God's purpose for your life. God has numbered your days. This not only means that He knows how many days you have; it also means that He has each day fully accounted for in detail according to His plan for you (See Jeremiah 29:11). God will fulfil every purpose He has for you, if you let Him. Quite often, however, the choices we make in life interrupt our course to the fulfilment of our God-given purpose.

What is it that you are passionate about and have a great desire to do towards helping to build the kingdom of God? Do you find yourself asking questions such as, "Who am I in God's Kingdom? Lord, what is it that You require of me?"

Let me share a few steps with you that will help you in discovering your God-given purpose:

Step 1: Go to God in prayer. Be intentional in seeking God on a daily basis. Build a relationship with Him and ask Him to order your steps. He will give you divine revelation of what He has called you to do. Be sincere in prayer as the Word of God says in Hebrews 11:6 that He is a rewarder of them who diligently seek Him.

Step 2: Indulge deeply in the Word of God. Psalm 119:105 declares, *"Thy word is a lamp unto my feet, and a light unto my path."* You should take the Word of God personally and practically, and habitually study it, so that you may see your way ahead and what lies in it. God's Word is sent to guide you, as you seek to discover and fulfil your God-given purpose on earth.

Step 3: Associate yourself with people who have the same desire. Proverbs 27:17 says, *"Iron sharpeneth iron; so a man sharpeneth the countenance of his friend."* When you associate with people who are desirous to fulfil their purpose, you will be motivated by their zeal and momentum.

Step 4: Nurture and use your gift to glorify God. Colossians 3:23 says, *"And whatsoever ye do, do it heartily, as to the Lord, and not unto men."* In order to nurture your gift, you must first accept the fact that they are God-given and must be nurtured and manifested according to His instructions. There is no room to think of your gifts as your own doing. Revelation 4:11 says, *"Thou art worthy, O Lord, to receive glory and honour and power: for thou hast created all things, and for thy pleasure they are and were created."* Once you acknowledge this fact, you are now ready to nurture your gift and use it to the glory of God. Nurturing these gifts requires absolute focus on the Word of God and prayer; it is in these that you receive divine instruction and build up spiritual muscle.

Step 5: You must act. The parable of the talents in Matthew 25:14-30 tells of a master who was leaving his house to travel. Before he departed, he entrusted his property to his servants. Each servant was given according to his ability. The servants who received more than one went and worked on it and made more on what he was given. However, the one who was given one talent hid it. God does not require us to bury and hide what He has blessed us with, then wait for His return. Rather, He expects us to sharpen what He has given us and use it to advance His kingdom. If you are diligent in sharpening your gift for service in God's kingdom, you will be rewarded accordingly.

Step 6: Align your desires to God's will. How can you tell the difference between your own desire and the will of God for you? Galatians 5:17 says, *"For the flesh lusteth against the Spirit, and the Spirit against the flesh: and these are contrary the one to the other: so that ye cannot do the things that ye would."* Your desires must feed your conscience with the Scriptures in order to make sure your heart's desires stay aligned with God's will for you. Spend time in prayer and ask God for revelation. He will reveal the answer to you through inward manifestation of the Holy Spirit, for example, discernment, and dreams and visions. Other times, He will use someone to deliver a confirmatory word for that season.

I can remember, years ago, I had this great desire to preach the Word of God. I had moments when I thought God had made a huge mistake to call me to be His mouthpiece because I was not outspoken enough; I was naturally very quiet and reserved. However, this great desire to serve God kept burning within me relentlessly. During moments of self-doubt, as I tried to hide away from this call, God would use people to speak over my life concerning preaching His Word, and it usually didn't take long for the prophecies to manifest. God will equip you for your calling, even when you believe you are not qualified for it.

"And he said unto them, Go ye into all the world, and preach the gospel to every creature." (Mark 16:15).

How to Keep the Spirit Man Alert
Spiritual Alertness

An answer to the greater call qualifies you as a soldier of Jesus Christ. In 2 Timothy 2:3, Paul challenged his disciple, Timothy, to discipline himself like a good soldier. As a soldier in the army of the Lord, the Bible gives the depiction of war. If you are going to be a good soldier for the cause of Christ, you must maintain keen awareness of what is taking place around you in the spiritual realm, in order for you to respond correctly. 1 Peter 5:8 declares; *"Be sober, be vigilant; because your adversary the devil, as a roaring lion, walketh about, seeking whom he may devour."*

Communication is very important in any battle. If the enemy can distort our communication with God, then we will be defeated in the fight. Ephesians 6:18 says: *"Praying always with all prayer and supplication in the Spirit and watching thereunto with all perseverance and supplication for all saints."* God requires us to be gatekeepers for our communities, homes, families, country and our fellow brethren.

A gatekeeper must be trustworthy and alert for any sign of trouble. If a gatekeeper becomes lax or losses focus on his duties, it can be very dangerous. In Ephesians 6, we are challenged to put on the armour of God. A necessary tool to this armour is the sword of the Spirit, which is the Word of God. According to Matthew 4:1-11, when Jesus was tempted by satan in the wilderness, it was the Word that He used to defeat him.

The Word of God is very important and is an effective tool or ingredient in allowing you to keep the spirit man alert.

Worship is another important tool. When we worship, we confuse the enemy and God responds. Acts 16:25 says: *"And at midnight Paul and Silas prayed, and sang praises unto God: and the prisoners heard them."* Paul and Silas were thrown into captivity, but by midnight, they knew the power of worship.

Fasting is also another tool. You must be willing to sacrifice the desires of the physical man in order to feed the spiritual man. Feeding the spirit man will build you up spiritually and activate a level of alertness. You must be on the alert, specifically to your weaknesses. Our adversary plays right along with our selfish desires (See 2 Corinthians 11:14).

Staying in God's Grace

You need the grace of God so you can effectively work in whatever area God has called you to in His Kingdom. The grace of God is the power and ability operating through us, with the help and influence of the Holy Spirit. The Holy Spirit helps us to stay sanctified and set apart; He helps us to overcome the lust of the flesh, lust of the eyes and pride of life (sin). If you are going to achieve real success in the Lord, and grow in His grace and knowledge, you need the power of His Holy Spirit to be working in and through you.

You will not be able to operate in your own strength as a child of God (believer). If you attempt to operate in your own strength, your desires, goals and aspirations are likely to be aborted by the attacks, schemes and tricks of the enemy. You must rely solely on God's power and leading to get where you need to be.

You can only reach your true divine destiny in the Lord, if His Holy Spirit is guiding and empowering you. 2 Peter 3:18 says, *"But grow in grace, and in the knowledge of our Lord and Saviour Jesus Christ. To him be glory both now and for ever. Amen."* If you allow God, through His Holy Spirit, to operate in and through you, then you will be well equipped to carry out His work/will in a mighty, powerful and effective way.

"Then he answered and spake unto me, saying, This is the word of the Lord unto Zerubbabel, saying, Not by might, nor by power, but by my spirit, saith the Lord of hosts." (Zechariah 4:6).

The grace of God is sufficient for you.

Intercession

According to the Oxford dictionary, intercession can be defined as: *the act of saying a prayer for somebody or something; a prayer that is said for somebody or something.*

In the Bible, we read about Moses, who had a huge task to lead the children of Israel out of Egypt. Therefore, he served as a mighty intercessor for them. Moses had to speak to God on behalf of the children of Israel, on the great exodus journey. His role and mission were divine and ordered by God.

The more we pray, according to the Word of God in a situation, the more we involve God in it.

"And Moses returned unto the Lord, and said, Oh, this people have sinned a great sin, and have made them gods of gold. Yet now, if thou wilt forgive their sin--; and if not, blot me, I pray thee, out of thy book which thou hast written." (Exodus 32:31-32).

I can identify with the story of Moses, the mighty intercessor, because there were times in my life that I had to become an intercessor for my family: my husband in particular. You must be alert and discerning when interceding on behalf of someone, because you will need to hear what God is saying to you about the person or the particular situation.

Here are a few tips to help you grow as an intercessor:

1. Be friends with God: become intimate with Him through meditating on His Word and engaging in intimate prayer, guided by the Holy Spirit. This will allow you to know His heart and pray according to His will.

2. Study the Word of God so you will be able to understand His will concerning a situation; then you will pray according to it, for example, praying or interceding for the sick. His Word declares in Isaiah 53:5 that by His stripes we are healed.

3. Develop a selfless heart: ministry is not about you, but it is about God and His kingdom. Be sincere in prayer. Cast down every selfish motive for intercession. It doesn't matter the ability of your vocabulary; God is not impressed with that. We must pray in spirit and in truth.

The Worship

Worship takes you into the presence of the Lord. He inhabits our worship. Exalt Him as Lord, give Him adoration. Let go of your own agenda so the Holy Spirit will flow, and you will enter into the inner courts of prayer.

Why do we worship Jesus? This is a crucial question that is sometimes asked. We worship Jesus because of His divinity. We worship Jesus because of His supremacy. We worship Jesus because of His humanity. We worship Jesus because of His humility.

My friend, do you really worship Jesus, or do you merely attend worship services every now and then? I urge you to worship Jesus. Give Him the worship that is due to Him. Romans 12:1 says: *"I beseech you therefore, brethren, by the mercies of God, that ye present your bodies a living sacrifice, holy, acceptable unto God, which is your reasonable service."* Echoing the words of Paul, I urge you to give your all to Him, who gave His all for you.

We are all faced with the struggle of not being able to worship our Creator when faced with some circumstances in life. Let me share one such experience I had. I remember when my child was sick for a period of one-year; sick to the point where I felt like giving up. Can you imagine your child, being an A-student in school, becoming so sick that she could not even remember how to write her name? Worship was hard for me then, but I had to comfort myself daily with the Word from Psalm 34. Worship is a lifestyle and must be done regardless of the circumstances we are going through. Here are a few reasons why praise and worship are important:

Worship allows us to put our focus on God. Isaiah 26:3 says: "Thou wilt keep him in perfect peace, whose mind is stayed on thee: because he trusteth in thee." True worship is based on the desire to honour God. It requires a personal revelation of God, as found in the Scriptures. Worship is not based on my likes or dislikes. It is not based on my personal preferences or priorities. It is a focus on Him.

Worship involves getting out of the way. We must learn to remove our worries, opinion, questions and ourselves, so we can worship with the appropriate honour. It is letting go. Sometimes, we get in the way of our own experience of genuine worship.

Worship involves personal sacrifice. This is showing God that you appreciate Him and all that He does for you.

Praise and worship sends the enemy running. Since praise manifests God's presence, we also realize that praise repels the presence of the enemy, satan. An atmosphere, which is filled with sincere worship and praise to God by humble and contrite hearts, is disgusting to the devil. He fears the power in the name of Jesus and flees from the Lord's habitation in praise. Psalm 50:23 says: "Whoso offereth praise glorifieth me: and to him that ordereth his conversation aright will I shew the salvation of God."

When the children of Judah found themselves outnumbered by the hostile armies of Ammon, Moab, and mount Seir, King Jehoshaphat and all the people sought the Lord for His help. The Lord assured the people that this would be His battle. He told them to go out against them, and He would do the fighting for them. So what did the children of Judah do? Being the people of "praise" (Judah actually means Praise), and knowing that God manifests His power through praise, they sent their army against their enemies, led by the praisers, shouting praises to Him and the enemies were smitten (See 2 Chronicles 20:22).

When God's people begin to praise His name, it sends the enemy running. I challenge you to become a person of praise, and you will experience the release of His power.

Conflict of the Heart

"Watch ye and pray, lest ye enter into temptation. The spirit truly is ready, but the flesh is weak." (Mark 14:38). This Scripture is just one of the numerous in the Bible, which illustrates a conflict between your own will and the will of God. Your own will is always in conflict with the will of God.

Many times, we find ourselves arguing against the calling of God on our lives, or even ignoring it all together, when it seems naturally difficult to align with it. God may even send obvious signals and evidence to us for this calling, but we find it difficult to surrender our own agenda to the agenda that God has for us.

As I engage you on this topic, "Conflict of the Heart," these are some crucial questions that you need to ask yourself:

- Are you walking in full obedience to the call of God for your life?

- Is God your strong foundation?

- Have you said yes to the call of God on your life? If not, what are your excuses for not committing to His will totally?

If your will and heart's desire is not aligned to God's will, you will operate contrary to God's agenda. If you have answered the greater call of Jesus Christ upon your life, you must come into full submission to the Lordship of Him and allow His will for your life to become priority.

Psalm 40:8 says, *"I delight to do thy will, O my God: yea, thy law is within my heart."*

Jeremiah 17:10 says, *"I the Lord search the heart, I try the reins, even to give every man according to his ways, and according to the fruit of his doings."*

- Are you called to be an Evangelist?
- Are you called to be a teacher of the Word?
- Are you called to the office of the Prophet?
- Is your ministry left unattended because you are busy chasing your own heart's desires?

I challenge you to walk in submission to the call of God upon your life. I challenge you to stir up the gift that He has blessed you with.

The Gift of the Holy Spirit is for all Believers

It is a common perception that the gift of the Holy Spirit is not for every believer. This perception, however, is contrary to the Word of God.

"And I will pray the Father, and he shall give you another Comforter, that he may abide with you for ever." (John 14:16).

The Holy Spirit is very important in the life of a believer and He plays many roles. In John Chapter 14, Jesus says the Holy Spirit will comfort us when we are hurting, and He will not leave us as orphans (See John 14:18). Jesus made a promise that the Holy Spirit will bring us peace (See John 14:27). The Holy Spirit will also help us to recall the things we have learned about God in His Word (See John 14:26). This means that the Holy Spirit will help us when we share our faith.

The Holy Spirit helps us in our weaknesses. *"Likewise the Spirit also helpeth our infirmities: for we know not what we should pray for as we ought: but the Spirit itself maketh intercession for us with groanings which cannot be uttered. And he that searcheth the hearts knoweth what is the mind of the Spirit, because he maketh intercession for the saints according to the will of God."* (Romans 8:26-27).

In John 14:26-28, Jesus refers to the Holy Spirit as a "helper" who will guide us in our everyday lives. One way He guides us is by convicting us of sin, and this is really a good thing. God wants us to get rid of the things in our lives and hearts that are not pleasing to Him. The only way to identify those things is by being convicted by the Spirit according to the Word of God in our hearts. The Spirit works the Word of God through our conscience, to make us aware of sin in our lives.

Notice the importance of the Word of God in the conviction of sin. This Word comes from what you consistently feed your spirit man, through reading and meditating on God's Word. It is only then that the Holy Spirit will lead you into all truth. You must also know that the Holy Spirit will not prompt you to do anything out of the will of God or His holy Scriptures. This therefore means that you must feed your spirit constantly with the Word of God, in order to discern the voice of the Holy Spirit and allow Him to guide you according to the Word.

How can you know if you are being led by the Holy Spirit? You will know by the fruit. Your life must bear the fruit of the Spirit, according to Galatians 5:22-23.

Tap into the Next Level

What is that one thing that may be preventing you from tapping into your next level?

In the Bible, the word "thorns" has been used to represent the following:

- Cares of the world
- Greed for riches/wealth
- Pleasures of the world

Could these things be so powerful in your heart that they hinder your spiritual progress?

Our flesh is the soil which favours the growth of thorns, and the only way to overcome it is by feeding our spirit with the Word of God.

Thorns are sometimes of God's appointment, serving as a leash to pride. *"And lest I should be exalted above measure through the abundance of the revelations, there was given to me a thorn in the flesh, the messenger of Satan to buffet me, lest I should be exalted above measure."* (2 Corinthians 12:7)

Questions: What is the one thing that is preventing you from tapping into your next level? Is it your business? Your Job? Your Spouse? Your children? Might you be too lazy to make the sacrifice that God requires of you?

It is my desire that your business, children, ministry, finances and everything you care about flourishes. However, your desire to flourish in these matters must not overshadow your desire to serve God and do His will.

We may become complacent and comfortable at times, but God keeps reminding us that we should step out of our comfort zones.

Prayer of Sanctification

My Father and Friend, I exalt and honour Your great name; You are awesome. You are Sovereign, You are the great and mighty God, the One who cleanses us from all our sins.

Father, I pray today, in the name of Jesus, that You will rid me of every sin, every weakness, and infiltration that the enemy uses to contaminate my mind. I pray, Abba, that as I seek You, and as I desire to grow in Your grace and knowledge, that You will cause Your anointing to purge me with the fire of Your Spirit; cause Your sanctification power to take a hold of my being, as I stay in Your will and walk in obedience to Your call. Your Word in Philippians 2:13 says that it is You who works in us to think and to act in accordance to Your will, in order to fulfil Your good purpose. Amen.

Prayer of Purification

Father, I worship and adore You. I *Shabbach* Your name for You are great, You are the most high Father. Your Word declares in Philippians 1:6 that You who begun a good work in me will perform it to completion unto the day of our Lord Jesus Christ.

Lord, I thank You for the work which You have begun in me. I set myself at the place where You will continue to purify me. Empty me of myself so that You will be able to fill me with Yourself. Lord, cause me to disconnect from everything that goes against your will and Word. This I ask today, in the name of Jesus Christ. Amen.

Prayer for Boldness

Father, You are worthy; You are awesome; You are great and mighty; You are sovereign. There is none to be compared to You. Lord, I acknowledge Your love, mercy and greatness. Wash me from all my sins and cleanse me, in the name of Jesus Christ. Lord, I come humbly before Your throne of grace, with the boldness of the Holy Spirit. Many times, I am plagued with fear, so today I give it to You.

I break the backbone of fear, in the name of Jesus Christ of Nazareth. I declare that fear is powerless, in the name of Jesus Christ of Nazareth. I declare that fear will be conquered by boldness, in the name of Jesus Christ.

Father, I pray for every person who is reading this prayer that has been paralysed by fear, to be freed, in the name of Jesus Christ. Father, replace their fear with boldness, for Your Word declares in 2 Timothy 1:7, that You have not given us the spirit of fear, but of love, of power and of a sound mind. Lord, thank You for giving Your people boldness; in the name of Jesus Christ I pray. Amen.

Prayer for Confidence

My Abba Father, I worship You; I honour and glorify Your name. You are awesome. You are worthy of our praises. I confess all my sins before You today. Wash me and cleanse me, in the name of Jesus Christ.

Father, many times I lack confidence but Your Word states in 1 John 5:14 that we should have confidence in approaching You, that if we ask anything according to Your will, You will hear us. Father, I believe Your Word and, today, I am declaring that the lack of self-confidence in my heart is destroyed in the name of Jesus Christ of Nazareth. Lord, You are my rock and fortress, and in You I will trust.

Lord, every person who is reading this prayer and suffering from a lack of confidence, I pray that You will begin to minister to their spirit. Lift their faith in You, Lord, so they will be engulfed with confidence from You. Lord, I thank You because I know You are restoring lives now, in the name of Jesus Christ I pray. Amen.

Prayer for Healing

I worship You, great Physician, the One who heals spirit, body and mind. Lord, today I humbly come to You. Forgive me of all my sins; wash me and cleanse me, in the name of Jesus Christ of Nazareth.

Father, many times I am afflicted in spirit, body and mind, but today, I ask that Your healing power will begin to manifest in my life. Lord, Your Word declares that by Your stripes, I am healed. I receive Your healing today, in the name of Jesus Christ of Nazareth.

I break the backbone of affliction, in the name of Jesus. Lord, Your Word says that whatever I bind on this earth, is already bound in heaven and whatever I loose on this earth, is already loosed in heaven. Today, I bind the stronghold of sickness in my body, mind and spirit and I declare that I am healed and made whole, in the name of Jesus Christ. Lord, I thank You for healing me, in the name of Jesus Christ I pray. Amen.

Prayer for Purpose

Heavenly Father, I worship You; I adore You and I exalt Your holy name. Your Word says that You inhabit the praises of Your people, so I praise You, Lord.

Father, forgive me of all my sins; wash and cleanse me, in the name of Jesus Christ. Lord, I know Your will for me is to walk in Your purpose for me. I align myself with Your Word to be the individual that You have called me to be.

Father, today I pray that as I strive to intentionally walk in my divine purpose, You will order my steps, guide me and take me unto the path that You want me to trod.

Father, without You I can do nothing; I would be a complete failure; I need Your direction. I pray against every demon that is assigned to abort my purpose: every destiny-killer, be destroyed now, in the name of Jesus Christ of Nazareth.

I declare today that I shall be intentional in walking in my purpose. I declare that I am not a failure. I declare that God is my source. I declare that I am blessed and highly favoured and no weapon that is formed against me shall prosper, in the name of Jesus Christ. Thank you, Abba Father. Amen.

Summary

"I press toward the mark for the prize of the high calling of God in Christ Jesus." (Philippians 3:14).

Looking back on my journey towards the purpose God has on my life is a humbling experience. I never imagined that I would be here to share and minister to you about stepping out to do God's will. When God calls you, no amount of running can outrun His call.

Your *Greater Call* started from before the foundation of the earth. Jeremiah 1:5 says, *"Before I formed thee in the belly I knew thee; and before thou camest forth out of the womb I sanctified thee, and I ordained thee a prophet unto the nations."* It is not an easy walk, but it is a fulfilling walk.

Jesus, at the last hour, felt the overwhelming burden of His call. He expressed how difficult it would be to carry out His assignment; He sweated blood, which showed He was experiencing the highest form of stress anyone could ever experience. He sought the Father three times about it. However, He obeyed the will of His Father. He now sits in the heavenly throne room as the Lord of lords, and the King of kings.

Your *Greater Call* may not appear fancy or easy, but just remember: Whatever God has called you to do, that gift He has placed within you, that is your *Greater Call*.

Are you ready for this *Greater Call?*

About the Author

Deneise Fearon is a licensed Minister, Author, Speaker and a certified International Empowerment and Spiritual Coach. Her coaching is faith-based and is guided by the Word of God. Deneise helps to guide women who are feeling stuck or stagnant in their growth, spiritual walk and faith, to discover their gifts and passion, so they can fulfil their God-given purpose.

Deneise has faced many challenges, but God gave her the strength and the willpower to fight. It is His grace that has sustained and kept her going. As a result of her faith in God, and stepping out intentionally in her purpose, she is now able to help others fight through challenging seasons of life as well.

For coaching and speaking engagements, you can contact Deneise at: deneisefearon@gmail.com

Made in the USA
Columbia, SC
02 August 2022

64359409R00043